Quick and Fun Learning Activities for Three-Year-Olds

Grace Jasmine

D1472151

Teacher Created Materials, Inc.

14002083

Illustrated by Sue Fullam and Jose L. Tapia
Cover Design by Larry Bauer
Images ©1996 PhotoDisc, Inc.

Made in U.S.A.

ISBN 1-55734-556-2

Order Number TCM 556

Table of Contents

Introduction

Is There a Three-Year-Old Pulling Your Arm Right Now?

If you are the parent of a three-year-old and you have picked up this book in a book store right now, there is a very good chance someone wishes you would hurry along and do what he or she wants you to do. That someone is your three-year-old!

If you are harried and hassled and don't have enough time in the day for anything, or if you haven't seen the inside of a locked bathroom in years, you might be the parent of a three-year-old!

If you say, "Put that down" and "Take that out of your mouth!" to perfect strangers, you might be the parent of a three-year-old. If you have heard the word "no!" more times than you care to remember (and sometimes you have even been the one saying it) you might be the parent of a three-year-old! And if you are, you have opened the right book!

How Can I Keep This Child Happy?

Keeping a three-year-old constantly content is asking the impossible. You can, however, provide your three-year-old with quality learning experiences at home and wherever you go, using the easy activities in this book. How do we know they work? I have tested each and every one of these activities with an expert in the field—an actual three-year-old, one who spent the duration of the writing of this book hanging from some part of my body.

Introduction (*cont.*)

Will This Book Work for My Three-Year Old and Me?

If you can answer yes to any of these questions, *Quick and Fun Learning Activities for Three-Year-Olds* will work for you and your active child.

1. Does your child show great interest in the world; is he/she constantly asking questions, getting into things, experimenting?

2. Does your child ask you many questions a day, show interest in others, and try to share experiences?

3. Is your child extremely active? Do you find yourself saying, "Sit down," "Don't touch," "Not right now," and "Take that out of your mouth" constantly?

4. Does a day with your child sometimes make you wish you were on a desert island—alone?

5. Do you worry that your child might not get all the quality learning activities you would wish for him or her at day care or for any other reason?

6. Do you want to maximize your time with your child and make playtime count as time to learn by playing?

7. Do you want to make the time you spend with your child more positive for both of you?

8. Is your child sometimes bossy, cranky, temperamental, or demanding?

If you can say "yes" to at least two of these questions, this book will help make living with and loving your three-year-old a wonderful experience for both of you!

Your Three-Year-Old

Is My Child Like Everyone Else's?

Yes and no. A three-year-old's normal development will vary greatly from child to child, and there is a lot of gray area between developmental milestones. It is normal to wonder how your own three-year-old measures up with other children his or her same age.

Some Days a Toddler, Some Days a Little Kid!

The National Association for the Education of Young Children (NAEYC) has developed a number of what they call "appropriate practices" regarding children from birth to age eight. Developmentally Appropriate Practices in Early Childhood Programs states, "Three-year-olds are no longer toddlers, but they will behave like toddlers at times; at other times their language and motor ability will deceptively mimic the four-year-old. The key is to maintain appropriate expectations. . . not expecting too little or too much of three-year-olds (1987, p. 47).

So, it's important to know what is reasonable and to set your expectations accordingly.

What to Expect

- Three-year-olds are developing their important independence skills. They may be angry and frustrated and need to "do it myself!"
- An angry, frustrated, or tired three-year-old may cry, thumb suck, or whine and need to be helped and comforted sometimes, just like a toddler.
- Three-year-olds may be in a period of slow growth. This often means your three-year-old won't have an appetite. Sometimes it seems as if they aren't eating anything, but, in fact, they are. Serve wholesome food in very small portions and try not to turn eating into a power struggle.
- Three-year-olds usually know how to share, but they won't always want to, nor is it always appropriate for them to have to. Everyone feels like privacy sometimes.
- Three-year-olds can become exhausted, tired, and cranky during the day. They often need afternoon naps.
- Three-year-olds need undirected activities every day and time to do them. A three-year-old's day should have plenty of self-directed and unstructured time.

Your Three-Year-Old *(cont.)*

- Three-year-olds need a play space indoors as well as outdoors and need to spend part of each day using large muscle groups for running, jumping, climbing, etc.
- Three-year-olds need to be exposed to books and read to every day.
- Three-year-olds do not need to learn the alphabet or numbers. With regular exposure to them, though, they will eventually learn and enjoy them.
- Three-year-olds need to feel safe. They need to be cuddled and told they are loved every day!
- Three-year-olds need to be talked with. They need to have conversations with caring, interested adults every day.
- Three-year-olds enjoy dramatic play, singing, and rhymes.
- Supervised television (especially videos and public television choices) often does much to enhance a three-year-old's experience and imagination and can be very positive.
- Three-year-olds are messy. They are not experts with napkins or with bathrooms. They get wet and muddy and dirty. They put things in their mouths when they shouldn't. They will put their fingers in electric outlets. They are often risk-takers.

How to Use This Book

Quick and Easy Overview

This book of activities has been designed for you to use quickly and easily with your three-year-old and to make the time you spend together a lot more enjoyable for both of you. The activities have been divided by topic, and each activity clearly lists the needed materials and offers easy-to-read, step-by-step instructions. The activities are easy to pull together with what you have around your house and are designed to be developmentally appropriate for your child. So, as well as being hassle free, they will help your child develop to his or her highest potential!

Getting Started

Begin by looking over the table of contents in this book. You will see that the sections are formed around everyday occurrences in the life of your three-year-old. There is no special situation you have to be in to make this work and not much that you will need to buy. The idea is to make your life and that of your three-year-old's easier to manage.

Before beginning, read "Your Three-Year-Old" and "Safety and Your Three-Year-Old." These brief sections will give you some quick insight about your child's development and some gentle reminders about safety in your home.

Sections Make Sense

Each section features an introduction explaining the section and offering some quick tips. The sections have been created to address some common everyday themes in daily life with your three-year-old.

- *Sick Days:* This section is filled with activities to help your child through days when he or she is home sick. They are easy and relaxing and will help brighten an otherwise unhappy day.
- *Holidays:* These are wonderful activities to make your three-year-old feel that he or she is part of the festivities, the activities in this section will help you enjoy the holidays with your child, even during stressful or exhausting moments.

How to Use This Book *(cont.)*

- *Busy Days:* These activities are for times when you and your child are on the run or when you need 15 minutes for yourself. They can help you survive hectic days more easily.
- *Mealtime Tricks:* Battles over food are sometimes very common with a three-year-old. The activities in this section will make it possible to enjoy mealtime and make it a pleasure to dine with your three-year-old (or at least less of a headache).
- *Temperamental Traveler:* On the road again? Getting there can be fun with travel activities that amuse your three-year-old. This section features portable activities to help you get there in one piece.
- *Nothing-to-Do Days:* Sometimes the very best days are the days with nothing to do. Nothing-to-Do activities are for days when you and your three-year-old have time to be creative, to explore, and to invent.
- *Summertime Fun:* The warm lazy days of summer make for great memories. This section has been designed to give you and your child some of the joy and relaxation associated with this time of year.

Dedicated to You and Your Happy Child

Raising a three-year-old is never easy. Some days it is downright frustrating, and other days it is the work we all love the most. This book is dedicated to loving parents everywhere who are making their children's world a happier, healthier, saner place.

Safety and Your Three-Year-Old

Playing Safe

No one has to tell the parents of a three-year-old that they must remain aware of their child's safety. All parents have some basic understanding of what precautions they need to take. The following tips are a general review about safety and your three-year-old, especially as they relate to activities in this book.

Safety Tips

- Outlets in your house or play area should have plastic outlet covers. If your child attends a day care or play facility, check the facility for protective outlet coverings.
- An adventurous child locked by mistake in a bathroom can mean tragedy. Remove bathroom locks in your house. Replace them as your child grows older.
- Large book cases, entertainment centers, or other large pieces of furniture should be bracketed to the wall. Three-year-olds are often excellent and speedy climbers.
- Store plastic bags and cleaning bags on high shelves or dispose of them after tying them so they cannot be opened and placed over little heads.
- Be aware that your child can pull a chair over to a cupboard and climb up. Three-year-olds are ingenious! Store medicine and cleaning supplies in locked containers.
- Be consistent about household rules. Be sure you communicate them to your child.
- Three-year-olds can open a front door and leave. They often can figure out dead bolts. Be aware of where your child is in your house.
- Watch the stove and oven. Explain to your child that they are only for adults to use.
- Assist your child with scissors, glue, or other potentially dangerous craft supplies. (Keep scissors and other materials out of reach.)
- When purchasing activity and art supplies, check for non-toxic labels.
- Always be aware of small pieces of craft supplies, coins, buttons, and small toys. Three-year-olds occasionally, while most of them know that they should not, put small objects in their mouths.
- Consider taking CPR training. It could save your child's life.
- Make your child water safe as soon as possible and remember he or she must still be watched while swimming or near water.
- Talk with your child about safety in the street. Practice crossing the street with your three-year-old. Teach your child he or she is not to go in the street unless holding an adult's hand.
- Discuss with your child about talking to strangers. There are several good videos, especially *Barney's Playing It Safe.*
- Show your child how to call 911 in an emergency. (Some three-year-olds will call to practice, so be aware of what will work best for your child.)
- Communicate! As your three-year-old becomes older and has more opportunities to be out in the world, the better you communicate with her, the safer and happier she will be.

Sick Days

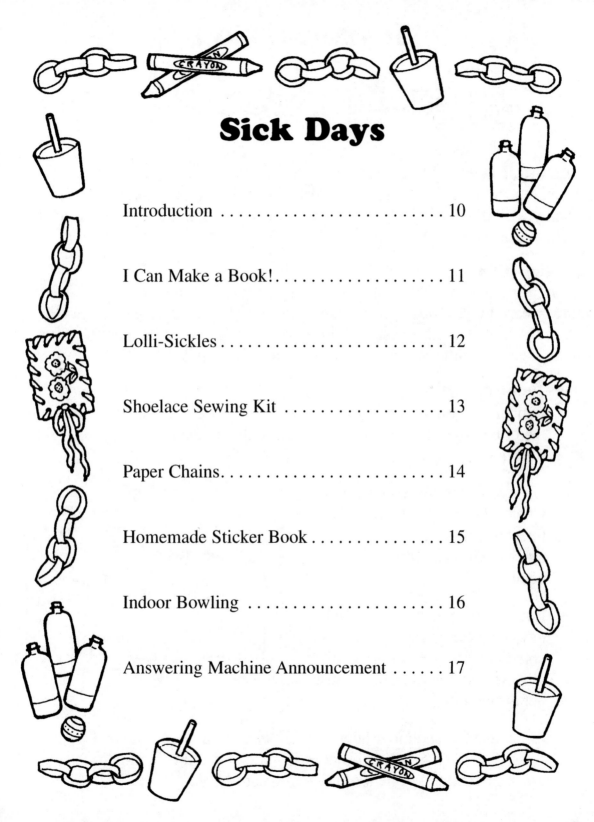

Introduction

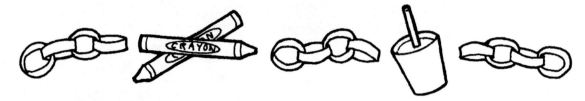

Mommy, I Feel Sick!

There is nothing worse than a cranky three-year-old, except, perhaps, a cranky, sick three-year-old. No one likes being sick, and it can be especially difficult for a three-year-old.

Making It Easier

The activities in this section have been designed to help you and your three-year-old have positive and as-happy-as-possible experiences when he or she is sick. Each of these activities is easy to do and will cheer up your three-year-old without making your life more complicated.

Tips for Sick Days

- Remember your child will most likely be harder to get along with today. Don't be upset if an activity isn't met with enthusiasm or if your child tires quickly.

- Give your three-year-old a choice when selecting an activity. Some times having just a tiny bit of control will help your child feel better.

- Lower your expectations. Sick days aren't days that you will feel completely organized or positive. Give yourself permission to just get through it.

- Empathize! Remember how you felt when you were little and were sick? We all remember instances in which an adult (mother, father, grandmother, etc.) took special loving care of us!

I Can Make a Book!

Activity

Often when your child is ill, she will become bored and restless more easily. You can get your three-year-old excited about making her own book of drawings. This activity will keep her happy and occupied while increasing her oral language and pre-reading skills.

To begin, encourage your child to make a number of pictures. Talk with her about how much fun it will be to take her pictures and make her very own book just like one of the books that you read to her.

Gather your child's drawings that you haven't wanted to throw away but are piling up around the house.

Show these pictures to your child and ask her to pick out the ones she wants in her book. Or, use them all.

Ask your child to tell you a story about each picture. Using a felt pen, write your child's words on the picture.

These are your child's first written stories, and this part of the activity will help her begin to make the pre-reading connection between the spoken and written word. Additionally, your three-year-old will tell you wonderful stories that will make this book a delightful keepsake for years to come.

Next, stack your child's pictures and staple them at the left margin with three staples. You can also punch holes in the pictures and place them in a three-ring binder or thread them with yarn and tie it in a bow. Ask your child to draw a picture for the cover of her book and help her write her name.

Give your child an opportunity to share her book with friends or other family members and add it to the books you read to her on a regular basis.

Grandparents love these books for gifts!

Materials

- Paper
- Crayons
- Stapler
- Felt pen
- Hole punch (Optional)
- Three-ring binder (Optional)
- Yarn (Optional)

Lolli-Sickles

Materials

- Small paper cups
- Apple juice
- Lollipops with sticks
- Freezer
- Cookie sheet or tray

Activity

This sick-day activity is easy and quick to do for a fretful three-year-old who has had to stay inside one too many days. You can help your child to make these quick and healthful treats, and at the same time also get him to drink more fluids while he is not feeling well.

Gather the ingredients and place them on a tray or cookie sheet. (This can even be done on a desk tray at a sickbed.) You will need one small paper cup, one lollipop, and several ounces of apple juice for each pop.

Help your child fill each paper cup with apple juice and place an unwrapped lollipop upside down inside the cup. The apple juice will cause the lollipop to partially melt and flavor the lolli-sickle.

Place the cups in the freezer. Check in 15–20 minutes and stand the sticks up straight in the cups. (Ice will be frozen enough by this time to enable you to stand the sticks up.)

Wait until the pops are frozen and serve them by loosening them from the cups. The lollipop stick will hold up the frozen treat, and then the lollipop can be eaten last.

Shoelace Sewing Kit

Materials

- Shoelaces or yarn
- White non-toxic glue
- Colorful pictures from old magazines
- Poster board or cardboard
- Hole punch
- Box

Activity

When your three-year-old is sick in bed, she can become very restless. Normal activities and toys might not be what the doctor ordered, and she will grow cranky because she can't play. Try this sewing kit activity for lots of in-bed fun. This activity is easy to prepare and can be used again and again. My daughter loves to use her sewing kit even when she is feeling fine. And, it is good for both girls and boys.

First, gather old magazines and cut out colorful pictures. Then glue the pictures onto poster board.

Punch evenly spaced holes around the entire edge of the picture board, about one inch (2.5 cm.) apart. On some of the boards, try making the holes farther apart to see what works best for your child.

Find a box large enough to hold the punched picture cards and the shoestrings. If you prefer not to use shoe strings, simply twist the ends of yarn with white glue and let them dry. This will form a pointed, strong end and make it easier to push the yarn strings through the card.

Show your three-year-old how to string the punched picture cards with the shoestrings or yarn. Store them to use again whenever your child is in the mood.

Try making a variety of picture cards, using magazine pictures that will appeal to your child. You can also use wrapping paper leftovers for colorful cards.

Paper Chains

- Construction paper
- White non-toxic glue
- Scissors
- Ruler

Activity

Nothing makes a three-year-old happier than decorating for a holiday or a birthday party. Why not ease the boredom of being sick by planning ahead for an exciting occasion?

Gather a variety of colors of construction paper. Cut a large number of strips. Strips of paper that are six inches long and ¾ of an inch wide (15 cm. x 1.88 cm.) work well for little hands.

Show your three-year-old how to glue a paper chain strip together by placing a tiny drop of glue on the end of a strip and holding it tight against the other end long enough for it to set.

Demonstrate and help her thread the second strip through the loop made by the first before gluing it.

Talk with your child as you go along about how nice and long her chain is becoming and how beautiful it will look as a holiday or party decoration.

Find a place to store the chain so your three-year-old can work on it for several days. This way she will be able to stop when she gets tired, and the activity will remain fun.

Display the paper chain in your child's room while she is sick and then put it away and save it for the planned occasion.

Homemade Sticker Book

Activities

Materials

- Photo album with clear plastic insert pages
- Stickers of all kinds

Being sick is never fun. When your three-year-old is well enough to take an interest in something but not well enough for normal play, making a sticker book is a wonderful activity. My daughter has a large photo album with magnetic cling pages that are usually peeled back to insert photos. Instead, she places her stickers right on the plastic surface of the pages. It works great, and she loves it!

First, find a photo album. Empty out an old one or buy a new one. They cost very little at discount stores.

Gather stickers for your child to add to her book. There are lots of inexpensive packages of stickers to be found in almost any store. Also, many stores have their own stickers that they will give away if you ask. Be aware of free sticker giveaways and also those offered with fast food. Put them away for this sick-day activity.

Help your child separate the stickers from their backs, and she will be able to stick them in her sticker book wherever she wants.

After your child fills her sticker book, she will enjoy looking at it again and again. You can also add pages when the book is full.

Indoor Bowling

Materials

- Large, lightweight plastic ball
- 10 plastic video cases or empty, plastic soft-drink bottles
- Hallway

Activity

Suppose your three-year-old is just getting over something contagious. You have had him with you constantly for over a week. You are frazzled. He feels great! He can't leave the house, and neither can you. What can you do with him? Now that you have stopped laughing hysterically, try indoor bowling. This activity was invented by a brilliant family friend, and while the materials are a little unorthodox, the relief you will feel from having something interesting for your bored three-year-old to do is well worth it!

Gather enough plastic video cases or empty plastic soda bottles to use for bowling pins. You can actually leave the videos inside their cases during the game. (The videos won't get damaged as the game is rather gentle.) Or, save up your empty plastic bottles. (Single-serving soda bottles will work as well as the larger ones.) Remember, bottle caps are a choking hazard. Be sure to remove them.

Find a hallway in your home to use. Close doors off the hallway so the ball won't get off track. Set up the plastic video cases or the empty plastic bottles the way they are set in a bowling alley. Many three-year-olds can help do this and will be able to re-set the pins. Practice with him a few times to show him how.

Bowl! Roll a lightweight plastic ball down the hallway, and you have your own indoor bowling alley! Take turns playing and see how the whole family does.

Encourage your child to set up the pins in a variety of different ways and see how this affects how many he can knock down. Have fun!

Answering Machine Announcement

Materials
- Answering machine

Activity

This is a quick activity that can be done again and again with little preparation—and children love it! In addition to it being a favorite activity of your three-year-old, your callers will think your child is the cutest, most talented child around. My daughter has made a variety of messages including holiday greetings and songs. We love it. (And if anyone is annoyed, we don't want to talk to them anyway!) This activity works especially well when a child is confined to the house and you are running out of ideas.

Talk with your three-year-old about making a recording for the answering machine. Play your current recording for her to listen to and ask her what she would like to say.

Next, let your child practice what she would like to say. Have her practice the basics of what you want on your machine, like, "Thank you for calling. Leave a message." You will have to help some three-year-olds a lot with this, and others will pick it up very quickly. This ability varies as much as it does with adults!

Try a recording. You will be able to play it back for your three-year-old so she can listen. You may have to do this a number of times to get one you are both happy with. Some of these recordings are priceless, and your child will be very proud of herself. (If you have an extra-special recording, add it to a permanent tape of your child's voice recordings.)

After the recording is finished, it's fun to sit around and wait until someone calls to see what they say.

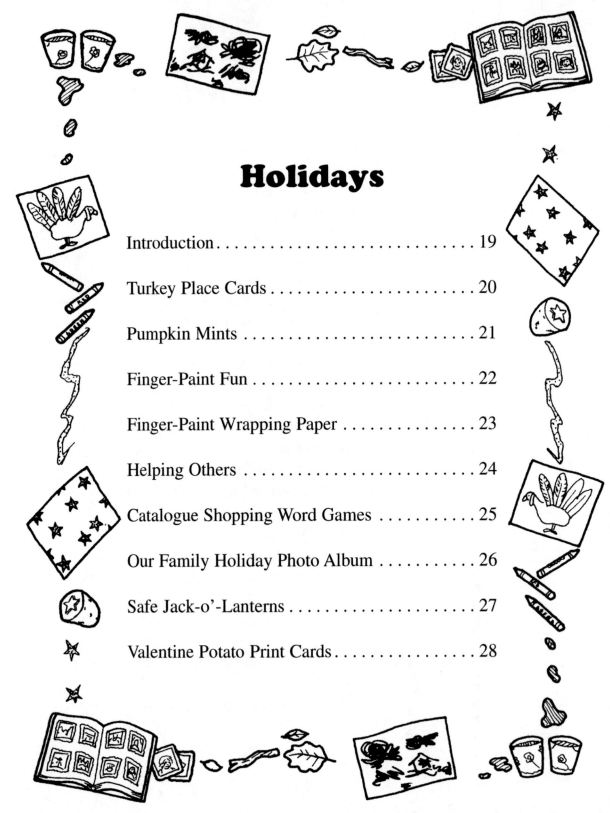

Holidays

Introduction

Happy, Harried Holidays

Oh, the holidays! When we think of them, do we think of happy times with family, friends, and children gathered around a table, faces shining? Or, do we think of arguments, children screaming, tears, and exhaustion? Holidays are a mixture. They bring out the best and the worst in all of us—including your three-year-old! Three-year-olds are in a period in which they are beginning to understand the meaning and the personal significance of what is going on around them. Their stress, over-stimulation, and excitement are a good thing—it means they are aware of their world and are beginning to understand it.

Making It Fun!

What can we do as parents to make holidays less stressful and more fun for all of us? First, realize that your three-year-old is going to get over-stimulated and excited, be too loud, and possibly cry or have a temper tantrum. This doesn't make your three-year-old worse than other three-year-olds; in fact, it makes your three-year-old normal. The activities in this section have been designed to assist you in turning holidays into magic memories with a minimum of hassle and stress.

Tips for Holidays

- Look over these activities before a holiday actually is upon you. Prepare for several of the activities and have the materials ready. This will make it possible for you to get your three-year-old happily involved as soon as you need to, thus preventing unhappy moments.
- Take a stress break! Get a family member to spend quality time with your three-year-old and so you can take a bath, a walk, or see a movie! You need time away from your child so that the time you spend together is as positive as possible.
- Relax! If it doesn't turn out exactly as you planned, in a hundred years, who will know? The activities in this section can be altered, just as holiday plans can be. The main thing is for you both to enjoy the day.

Turkey Place Cards

Materials

- Colored construction paper
- Glue stick or white glue (non-toxic)
- Scissors
- Markers or crayons

Activity

Making place cards for your Thanksgiving table is a fun way to get your three-year-old involved in your festivities and is uncomplicated enough to be done while you rest after your turkey is in the oven! My three-year-old was thrilled to be able to show our guests her contribution to our Thanksgiving table, and everyone had a handmade remembrance of a warm and wonderful Thanksgiving!

Clear an easy-to-reach flat surface for you and your child to use. Gather all the materials and place them on the table. Use a glue stick and crayons, rather than white glue and markers, if you are concerned about a quick cleanup for messy fingers.

Pre-cut some turkey feathers in a variety of colors; each turkey place card will need four feathers. Remember, these don't need to be perfect. Have your child begin to draw details on the feathers while you get the rest of the project ready. Next, have your child place her hand on a piece of construction paper and trace it for a turkey body pattern. Cut one hand out of colored construction paper for each place card.

Have your child glue one feather on each of the finger sections of the body and draw a face on the thumb.

Fold a separate piece of construction paper in fourths to use as a base. Glue the finished turkey on the place card and help your child label each one with a guest's name.

Note: Don't be surprised if at the end of the activity you are doing all the work, including the labeling. The main idea is for both of you to have some quality time on a busy day and for your child to have the thrill of being part of your Thanksgiving celebration!

Pumpkin Mints

Materials

- ¼ cup (60 mL) of milk
- 4 teaspoons (20 mL) of butter
- 3 ¼ cup (780 mL) of powdered sugar
- 2 to 3 drops of peppermint extract
- Green, red, and yellow food coloring
- Aprons or old shirts
- Paper towels
- 2 bowls
- Saucepan
- Fork
- Serving plate

Activity

Most recipes that you might attempt with your three-year-old are frustrating and unsuccessful. But not this one! Making these pumpkin mints is an easy and fun hands-on cooking experience that three-year-olds can really help with successfully. The result is wonderfully tasty after-dinner mints that your three-year-old will have made himself for Halloween or Thanksgiving celebrations!

The adult should heat the milk and butter. Add the powdered sugar and mix it together. Add the drops of peppermint extract.

Next, help your child knead the mixture with clean hands until the candy is a smooth ball. Take ⅛ of the mixture and mix it with several drops of green food coloring for the stems. Knead this again to make the color even. Put it in a covered container.

Help your child knead the rest of the candy with equal parts of red and yellow food coloring to make a nice pumpkin color.

Have your child roll small balls of orange candy into pumpkins and place them on the serving plate. Add a small piece of green candy for the stem. (Use a fork to make the grooves of a pumpkin.)

Now you're ready to serve and enjoy! These will stay nice for a day or two. They can be served as after-dinner mints and also make wonderful table decorations.

Finger-Paint Fun

Materials

- Area for painting
- Finger-painting paper
- Newspaper
- Poster or finger paints
- Paper towels
- Soap, water, and old clothes
- Two paper cups or plastic containers
- Two plastic spoons
- Sponge
- Clothespins
- Liquid laundry starch (Optional)

Activity

Three-year-olds love to finger paint, and hands-on activities (even messy ones) are excellent for your child's healthy development. Relax, enjoy, and put on your oldest sweatshirt!

To begin, clear an outside work space with a comfortable place for you and your child to sit. Almost any space you can easily clean up will work. Covering the work area with a thick pad of newspaper helps soak up the water.

Pour (or spoon) paint into paper cups or containers. Use just one or two colors for your painting. Too many colors may produce a muddy-looking result! Also, if you are using poster paint, mix it with some liquid laundry starch. The paint spreads better.

Place the finger-paint paper on the working surface. Wet the paper with a sponge to keep the paper from flying away and to make it easier to spread the paint. Show your child how to make different designs or simple shapes, using the side of the hand as well as the fingers.

Let your child make a number of pictures. As the pictures are completed, you can use clothespins to pin them to a fence (or even a bush) to dry.

Finger-Paint Wrapping Paper

Materials

- Area for painting
- Finger-painting paper
- Newspaper
- Poster or finger paints
- Paper towels
- Soap, water, and old clothes
- Two paper cups or plastic containers
- Two plastic spoons
- Sponge
- Clothespins
- Materials for moving paint around: leaves, blunt sticks, pieces of sponge, etc.

Activity

Your three-year-old will love making his very own wrapping paper and helping to wrap holiday presents for very special people in his life.

Use the information on page 22 to prepare the work area, the containers of finger paint, and the paper.

After your child has used his hands to create designs on the paper, encourage him to experiment with other materials for moving the paint around. You can even dip fruit, such as lemons and oranges, into the paint and make fruit-print designs!

Let your child create several paintings. After the paintings are dry, press them under books or any other heavy object to flatten and smooth them for use as wrapping paper. Make paper with a holiday theme by using different colors. For example, use red and green paints for Christmas paper or blue paint for Hanukkah. Use pink or red for Valentine's Day and pastels for Easter or special birthdays.

Your child will be able to tell people that he made the beautiful paper himself!

Helping Others— Teaching Giving and Sharing

Materials

- Gift box
- Tape
- Scissors
- Construction paper
- Crayons
- Wrapping paper
- Bows

Activity

Teaching children to give and to share is an important task and one that can be started far earlier than age three. However, three-year-olds love to give presents and can take part in a lot of the planning and carrying out of gift giving. My three-year-old loves to give gifts, and even though she sometimes confides what the secret is before the gift is opened, the experience is fun for all of us!

First, talk about giving and sharing with your child. A holiday makes a great time to do this, but you can give presents anytime. Sometimes it is even more exciting to give an unexpected gift.

Gather the materials from around the house (or a discount or craft store) with your child. This is part of the fun. You may wish to create your own wrapping paper and keep it on hand. (Any picture your child makes can be used as wrapping paper.)

Talk with your child about what she will give as the gift and to whom she would like to give it. Then, either make or buy a small gift. (Remember, gifts don't have to cost anything, or they can be very inexpensive. It's the thought that counts!)

Help your child select, wrap, and present her gift. Talk about what fun it is every step of the way!

Though three-year-olds can really help a lot with this activity, remember to keep sharp scissors out of the way of little hands.

Catalogue Shopping Word Games

Materials

- Old catalogues
- Pencils, pens, or crayons

Activity

Three-year-olds have a natural curiosity about language and written communication. You can help your child to become familiar with letters and words and have an interesting, productive, and (even better!) no-preparation-required activity to use anytime.

Simply gather some old catalogues. You can use any kind of catalogue that might appeal to your child. You might want to let your child choose his favorite from a number you collect.

Look at the catalogue with your child. Ask what your child likes best on every page. Talk about color, size, cost, and what the items are used for. Read the words about each item for your child. If your child can recognize letters, point to a letter and ask him to name it. You can do the same thing with numbers. Show your child words and relate the words to the pictures he sees.

Re-read the same catalogue with your child often. While this may seem boring to you, a three-year-old loves to do this and will be excited about what he recognizes and remembers as he re-reads the catalogue. Try doing it different ways. Ask him to explain the pictures to you or to find a special part of the catalogue.

You will find that catalogue shopping has never been so much fun!

Our Family Holiday Photo Album

Materials

- Disposable camera or already-developed photos
- Empty photo album

Activity

Remembering special occasions is important to three-year-olds. The ability to recall events and remember specifics about events is part of your child's healthy mental development. If you have a large and extended family, creating and using a photo album with your child will help her to remember family—even when they can't always be there!

Decide whether you want to actually take pictures with your child or put already-developed pictures in a photo album. If you decide to take them, embark on a fun-filled day of smiling and camera-clicking before moving on.

With your child, look over the photos you have gathered or taken and developed. Let her select pictures to place in the photo album. (Be prepared to assist her with putting the pictures in the album.)

Look at the album again and again with your child and let her share the photo album with other family members and friends. This will help your child develop many of the skills associated with verbal (and later) written language.

From time to time, add to the photo album. Make a ritual of taking pictures on holidays and then entering the new pictures in the photo album. This way your child will have a chronological record of events in her life that she created herself!

Safe Jack-o'-Lanterns

Materials

- Construction paper
- Tape
- Scissors
- A pumpkin
- Felt pens or crayons

Activity

One of the best parts of Halloween is making and displaying a jack-o'-lantern. Three-year-olds love to see them; however, they are dangerous for little fingers. Many children get burned every year! This safe jack-o'-lantern activity will give you a wonderful alternative to try with your three-year-old. My daughter loves this activity since she can change her jack-o'-lantern's face again and again!

Gather the art materials for this activity and then make going to get the pumpkin part of the fun. Many cities have pumpkin patches in October where you can take your three-year-old and select your own pumpkin together.

When you get home with your pumpkin, explain to your three-year-old that he is going to use construction paper to draw eyes, a nose, and a mouth for the pumpkin.

After your child has finished the eyes, nose, and mouth for his pumpkin, cut them out. (Remember to keep sharp scissors out of little hands.) Place a rolled piece of tape on the back of each piece. This will stick both to the paper and to the pumpkin. Help your child affix his construction paper face pieces to the pumpkin. Encourage him to try different designs and make other kinds of faces, too.

Note: Suggest to your child that he try faces for his pumpkin that are sad, happy, angry, tired, funny, scared, etc. Talk about what each of these feelings is like and when he feels these different emotions.

Valentine Potato Print Cards

Materials

- White or pink paper
- Red poster paint
- Newspaper
- Paper towels
- Sponge
- Potatoes
- Sharp knife (for the adult)
- pen or marker

Activity

Saying "I love you" is a wonderful part of life! And three-year-olds love to say it and to share affection with those they love, too! This easy-to-make Valentine potato print card will be fun for your child, as well as something she can really do herself.

Prepare the potato before beginning this activity with your child. First, cut the potato in half, and then, using a pen, trace a heart on the flat, cut surface. Carve around the heart-shaped pattern until it stands out from the potato. (You may wish to prepare several potatoes so you can both try the activity at once.)

Fold the paper into a card and place it on newspaper before you begin the printing. Pour poster paint into a pie plate so that it is easy to dip the potato into the paint without spills. Now begin to print. Your child will be able to do this part of the activity with little assistance. However, be aware that this is a messy activity, and have paper towels and a damp sponge nearby.

When the card is dry, ask your child to tell you what she wants you to write inside it. Write her message in the card and let her deliver it herself for a special Valentine treat.

This potato-heart print can also make lovely wrapping paper.

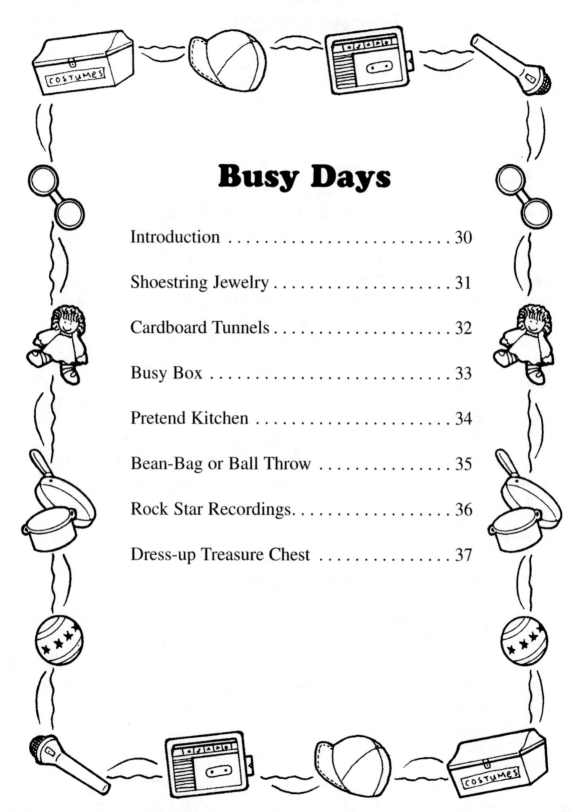

Busy Days

Introduction

I'm Late!

Everyone has too much to do. Most parents of three-year-olds are very busy people. How can you make your time with your three-year-old quality time, even if sometimes the time that you have is short? The activities in this section have been designed in two ways. First, they can be done on the run. Several activities have been designed to do while on the way to some place or in short time periods. Second, there are several activities that will give *you* some time. They have been designed to give your three-year-old something to do that is interesting and absorbing so you can have a few minutes to concentrate on something else (or maybe even put your feet up for a few seconds).

Quick Quality Time

When you and your child only have a few minutes, remember to concentrate on what is happy. Sometimes the best thing to do with your three-year-old for a few minutes is cuddle and talk. We all can use quick, cuddly, quality time.

Tips for Busy Days

- Plan ahead. Look over the activities in this section and commit some to memory to use when you and your three-year-old are on the run.
- Prioritize. When you are busy, remember what is important. It is more important for you and your child to have a happy and connected five minutes than it is for you to complete an activity. Be flexible and aware of your child's needs.
- Enjoy yourself. Take time with your three-year-old on a busy day to just stop for a second. Look at a flower. Smell a rose. Watch the clouds for a moment. Or just hug!

Shoestring Jewelry

Materials

- Several new shoestrings
- Stringable pasta
- Food coloring
- Small containers with lids
- Brown lunch bags
- Box with lid
- Cookie sheet
- Paper towels
- Scissors

Activity

Ever need a couple of minutes without distractions? When your three-year-old makes shoestring jewelry, you might be able to claim a minute or two for yourself. This jewelry uses shoestrings rather than needles and thread and can be used again and again. Three-year-olds love to string their own jewelry and enjoy wearing their creations. Grandmothers love these homemade presents, too.

Buy a variety of stringable pasta. Some varieties that will work well for this activity include salad macaroni (ditalini), elbow, ziti, penne, rigatoni, and wagon wheels (rotelle). When selecting pasta that can be used for this activity, remember your child has to be able to put string through the pieces.

Next, get a small plastic container to store each kind of pasta for your child's shoestring jewelry kit. You can use leftover, clean margarine tubs with lids for this purpose. Use a box that has a lid and is large enough for all the materials, and you will have a game you can take out and put away easily.

Color the pasta to make the jewelry game more interesting by dripping several drops of food coloring into a brown paper bag containing the pasta you are coloring. Close and shake the bag. Pour the colored pasta on a paper-towel-covered cookie sheet to dry.

Using the pasta and several shoestrings, show your child how to string jewelry. Tie large knots in one end of each shoestring. Use scissors to cut shoestrings to different lengths for bracelets, necklaces, etc. (It will help to keep one plastic end on a string to serve as a needle.)

Cardboard Tunnels

Materials

- Large cardboard boxes
- Large playing space
- Masking or packing tape (Optional)

Activity

I discovered this tunnel game while moving into our new house. Rather than tell my restless child to get away from the moving boxes again, we constructed a series of play tunnels that made her moving day a lot of fun. This activity can be done any day, and boxes can be stored and used again whenever you wish.

Just gather empty boxes that are big enough for your child to crawl through.

Clear a playing space that is large enough for you to place a number of boxes end to end. The tunnel you create doesn't have to be a straight one but can twist and curve according to the playing space you have. (This also makes it more interesting.)

Have your three-year-old help you decide how to set up the tunnels and then let him try it to see if it works. You can tape the flaps of the boxes together, but it isn't necessary.

Let your child have fun experimenting with the tunnel and moving the boxes around to make different shapes. This activity will keep him entertained for quite a bit of time, maybe even long enough for you to pack or unpack a box!

Store folded boxes in a garage, a large closet, or under a bed to use again to play tunnels.

Also, you can give your child crayons to decorate the boxes inside and out. Invite favorite dolls or stuffed animals on a tunnel tour, too.

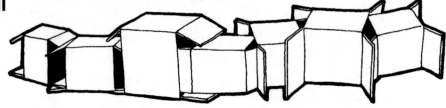

Busy Box

Materials

- Action figures or other small toys
- A suitable container (See suggestions below.)

Activity

When you and your three-year-old are on your way somewhere where you will have to wait, it is good to be prepared. Waiting with a three-year-old can be one of life's most exhausting experiences. This homemade "Busy Box" will help you keep your child occupied wherever you have to wait. My daughter is naturally curious and active, and this activity has helped us take care of business many times!

Find a plastic box with a lid that is small enough for your child to carry and large enough to hold the items you want to put inside. Several makers of baby wipes package their wipes in resealable, reusable containers that they advertise as storage boxes. These containers work well for this activity. (Another idea is to use a plastic lunch box or a child-size backpack.)

Next, go through your child's small toys, like action figures and fast-food giveaways. Select a few favorites for the "Busy Box." Use caution, however. DO NOT put in anything that can spill, stain, or that isn't well made or safe. Explain that these are going to be special toys to be used only in special situations, such as waiting in offices or on long car trips.

Consider adding a few surprises to the box. You might add a small package of crayons and a coloring book, or several small, wrapped lollipops. (You can even buy sugar-free ones.)

Take the "Busy Box" along when you and your child have to wait. This box of goodies and activities will keep her busy for a long time. Let her make suggestions about what kinds of things she would like in the box and change the contents occasionally.

Pretend Kitchen

Materials

- Pots and pans
- Unbreakable kitchen tools
- Cardboard box
- Large-tipped felt pens

Activity

Three-year-olds love kitchens! They love to play with the real items Mommy or Daddy use. This kitchen activity makes an interesting reusable kitchen play set. I found that my daughter enjoys using real kitchen tools in the play kitchen I made for her far more than a purchased kitchen that she uses only occasionally.

Select items from your kitchen that are safe, unbreakable, and not near and dear to your heart. Make sure items can't be swallowed, are in good repair, and have no sharp edges. You will have a sense of what is safe for your three-year-old—some three-year-olds still put everything in their mouths; others do not.

On the flat-bottom surface of a large cardboard box, draw a stove top, using large-tipped felt pens. (Your child doesn't need a professional job; circles that can be used as pretend burners will do nicely.) Make an oven by cutting a door in the side of the box. Use your imagination here and  remember your child will be far better at imagining that this is an oven/stove than you will.

Three-year-olds love this game and will gladly bake pretend pies or cakes or cook dinner for a doll family. Be prepared to sample pretend foods and "ohh" and "ahh" over pretend creations. (All cooks like praise!)

The play kitchen also presents a good opportunity to teach and explain some basic rules about cooking and kitchen safety.

Bean-Bag or Ball Throw

Materials

- Pots, pans, or empty baskets
- Small toy balls or bean bags
- Play space

Activity

This activity was invented by a three-year-old. Make a throwing game with things you already have around the house. The sky is the limit. Throwing a small ball or a bean bag and aiming at a target will help your child develop important large and small muscle group coordination—an important part of your child's healthy physical development. When I play this game with my daughter, she always wins!

Gather a variety of containers from around your house. Practically anything will work. You can use pots, pans, plastic containers, boxes of different sizes, plastic bowls, etc.—whatever is on hand.

Next, gather the balls that your child already has that are small enough to fit into the containers. If you wish, you can substitute bean bags or use both.

Set up a throwing game. Set several bowls in a row at different distances. You can experiment with this part of the game or let your child set it up.

Demonstrate tossing the ball for your three-year-old. Have him practice the game and then take turns throwing. (You may find it is a pretty even game!) Use this activity as an opportunity to count. For example, throw the ball three times and count "one, two, three," etc.

Be creative! You can make up a variety of different games or let your three-year-old make up a game and teach it to you. This experience will increase your child's oral language and thinking skills.

Rock Star Recordings

Materials
- Tape recorder with microphone
- Blank cassette tapes

Activity

Kids love music! And children from a very early age are interested in music and singing. Inspire your three-year-old to use her singing voice to make her own voice recordings. These recordings are great learning experiences for your child. They provide hours of entertainment and make wonderful keepsakes or presents.

Get out your tape recorder and blank cassette tapes. You will find it easier for your child if there is no plug or outlet involved, so use the battery option, if you have one, for safer and less complicated operation. (There are also kid-friendly tape recorders made by several toy companies that specialize in toys for preschoolers.)

Show your three-year-old how to use the record function. You will have to put the cassette in and show her how to turn it on. Eventually, many three-year-olds can master putting in their own tape and turning on their own tape recorder.

Practice singing songs with your child. When she is ready to record, encourage her to record the song a number of times. Play back the recording and listen to it together. (Remember there is no right way with this. The idea is to create and have fun.)

Encourage your three-year-old to share her recording with other family members, give it as a gift, or use it as a holiday greeting.

As an alternative, find other interesting things to record. Help your three-year-old make a recorded letter to Grandma or Grandpa. Let everyone say hello, even your dog and cat. Grandparents are sure to love it!

Dress-up Treasure Chest

Materials

- Box with lid
- Old clothes or costumes

Activity

Pretending is an important part of your three-year-old's life. The ability to create and pretend is a vital part of the development of her mind. Make pretend time even more interesting with this "Dress-up Treasure Chest." It's not expensive, and you can use things you already have. Also, you can add to it or change it easily.

Find a sturdy container to use for a costume box. Look through your old clothes and the clothes of other family members to find interesting pieces to put in it. Things like hats, shoes, party clothes, and grown-up clothes work great. Add leftover Halloween costumes, too. Think about clothes that your child could wear to pretend she is a certain profession or a fantasy character. Things that you might not ordinarily think of can make wonderful fantasy costumes. For example, a scarf can be many things: an Arabian Nights headdress, a skirt, a toga, a horse's mane, and much more!

Get your three-year-old involved in filling the costume box. Talk about the things you are putting in it. Listen to her ideas because she will have many.

Place the costume box where your child can have access to it whenever she wishes, and suggest on days when she has nothing to do that she use her costume box to have a pretend adventure.

Get involved with your child in pretend adventures. You can play different parts and join in on many pretend activities.

Note: Ask your friends and relatives for additions to the costume box. And don't forget to think about its contents when dress-up occasions (like Halloween) come around.

Mealtime Tricks

Introduction

Your Three-Year-Old and Eating

Fussy! Demanding! Hard to get along with! No, not your boss—your three-year-old at mealtime. Three-year-olds are learning about their own power and their own ability to choose. And while this may seem wonderful in theory, sometimes it isn't so wonderful when your tiny tyrant is screaming and crying over a plate of vegetables. The activities in this section have been designed to bring the fun back into mealtime and stop the power struggle.

Expectations and Reality

Three-year-olds are fussy about what they eat. And experts agree that eating what seems to be a very small amount, not finishing what they have served to them, or completely refusing many foods are all normal. We all dislike certain foods; it's a matter of preference in many situations. So, make mealtime pleasant by lowering your expectations to fit the normal development of a three-year-old. Expect him to often dislike what you serve. (This isn't an insult. He is three!) Expect your child to spill milk and to act inappropriately. Gently remind and model, and keep your three-year-old out of no-win situations. There is plenty of time for fine dining—later!

Tips for Mealtime Tricks

- Serve a variety of healthful foods and let your child sample them. Serve foods that are possible to eat with fingers as well as those that must be eaten with forks and spoons. Your child will enjoy the break of practicing with his fork and spoon to pick up an apple slice or a carrot stick.
- Don't get into a power struggle. If you have to win, it will make you very tired.
- When eating out, choose kid-friendly restaurants. Then, if your child acts his age, everyone who is dining will be prepared. Fast-food places are a great place for trying out table manners in public.

Very Merry Unbirthday

Materials

- Party hats
- Candles
- Cake
- Balloons
- Art materials
- Leftover party supplies
- Dress-up clothes

Activity

Sometimes we all need a special day. You can make any lunch or dinner into an impromptu unbirthday party and get your three-year-old involved in the fun. With a cake, candles, and make-them-yourself party hats, you can make an occasion for your three-year-old that will make any day more memorable and fun.

Talk about the idea of an unbirthday with your child. If your child is not familiar with the movie *Alice in Wonderland*, you may want to rent or buy the video, or take out a written-for-small-children edition of this classic. Talk about how an unbirthday is a celebration you can have any time you want to have a party!

Decide with your child what kind of party you will have. Make a cake or buy one from the store or even put candles on a store-bought cupcake for an instant unbirthday cake. (Three-year-olds love to be included in the fun and will love to help frost a cake or pick out the perfect birthday candles.)

Next, make or buy party hats. Simple hats can be made by taping a piece of construction paper in a cone shape and decorating with crayons, a glue stick, and glitter.

Have your unbirthday party. Play games, sing songs, light candles, and let your three-year-old make the wish!

It is also fun to learn and sing "A Very Merry Unbirthday" from Disney's *Alice in Wonderland*.

Another option is to make this an occasion for your three-year-old to consider the needs of others by preparing a surprise unbirthday party for another member of the family who needs a celebration for one reason or another. Small children take great delight in making the people they love happy.

Funny-Face Sandwiches

Materials

- Bread
- Peanut butter
- Raisins
- Shredded coconut
- Apple and banana slices
- Carrot sticks
- Butter knife
- Serving tray

Activity

Ever have trouble getting your three-year-old to eat? After you are able to stop laughing, help your child become excited about mealtime by making funny-face sandwiches. My three-year-old loves to make her own funny face sandwiches, and she actually eats them. I love this activity because it keeps her busy for a half-hour, and I can have a cup of coffee and my own time out.

Place the ingredients for sandwich faces on a tray or a cookie sheet. This will help you to keep the activity more organized and help with cleanup. Cut up the foods that will be difficult for your child to handle, like the apple slices, etc.

Next, place a slice of bread on a plate and show your child the sandwich illustrations below. Help her decide what kind of face she would like to make. Be available to help her as needed as she makes her sandwich.

Serve juice or milk and the rest of the carrot sticks, and your child will have a healthful, funny, and interesting lunch.

Let your child make sandwich faces whenever you need a lunchtime lift. You can even use the same supplies for breakfast. Let your child create a pancake or toast face in the same way!

ABC Placemats

Materials

- Construction paper or paper placemat
- Felt pens or crayons
- Breakfast, lunch, or dinner

Activity

Sometimes the best thing to do to make a meal go smoothly is to use a distraction. Turning a placemat into an alphabet game is an easy and interesting way to keep your child occupied during a meal. "ABC Placemats" will keep your child entertained while providing exposure to letters and words—an important pre-reading skill. This activity has made it possible for my family to actually make it through an entire restaurant dinner, and the result for my daughter has been, over time, that she knows the alphabet!

This activity can be done easily at home or in any restaurant with disposable paper placemats. (At home, use a clean piece of construction paper.) Write a different letter of the alphabet every day. Begin with the letter "A." Talk with your child about the letter "A." If you are at home, begin the morning by singing the alphabet song. (If you are in a restaurant, you may wish to forgo singing the alphabet song unless you are brave and it is a casual atmosphere.)

Give your child several crayons, and as you discuss the letter and words that begin with the letter, suggest to him that he draw an apple or an ant or whatever object he can associate with the letter.

If your child is interested, show him how to draw the letter. Let him use the placemat to practice the shape of the letter. Show him both the uppercase and the lowercase printing of the letter.

Write out the entire alphabet for your child and say the name of each letter as you point to it. Let your child show you the letters he recognizes. (The more you do this with him, the more letters he will begin to recognize.)

As a variation on this theme, turn the letters into funny

ABC Placemats *(cont.)*

pictures. "A" can easily become a stick figure. "S" can turn into a snake. "O" is a natural for a happy face or a sun. The artistic adults in your family may decide this is as much fun for them as it is for your three-year-old. (And most restaurants will supply extra placemats, if you need them.) Just be sure to take the placemat home to look at later!

As an alternative, try the same activity with numbers. For example, write the number 2 and then draw sets of things that come in twos, like shoes, hands, feet, etc. Write the numbers from one to ten on your child's placemat and draw sets of dots to go with them. (If anyone in your party is feeling creative, the number 8 makes the foundation for a great snowman.)

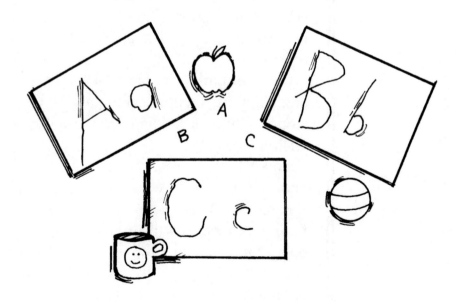

Toddler Fruit Salad

Materials

- Apple and banana slices
- Raisins
- Tiny marshmallows
- Finger-food cereal
- Large spoon
- Small bowls or plates
- Large bowl

Activity

This "Toddler Fruit Salad" is a healthful, fun-to-make salad that your three-year-old will be able to make. Somehow, when children are involved with food preparation, they have more interest in eating. Use the simple recipe here or create your own versions with what you have on hand in your kitchen. My daughter loves to make this easy fruit salad, and she will even take a bite!

Place small bowls, or paper or plastic plates, of already cut-up ingredients on a tray. (Three-year-olds are often frustrated if they have to cut up ingredients. Making the salad might become a stressful event.)

Use a table that your child can easily reach and a comfortable chair as a work space. (Food preparation works better with small children when they are organized and sitting down.)

Let your child combine the ingredients and mix the salad with a spoon. Talk with your child about each ingredient and give her positive feedback about the kind of job she is doing.

Let your child serve herself (and also you). Sit down and enjoy her creation. Prepare the rest of lunch to go along with the salad and serve it at the same time, if you wish.

You can also have your child make this special fruit salad for family parties. It will be a chance to share the skill with family members.

Gelatin Sky

Materials
- Blue gelatin
- Large marshmallows
- Rectangular plastic container or gelatin mold

Activity

Three-year-olds love gelatin! It looks so funny when it wiggles! And it is so much fun to eat! This "Gelatin Sky" is an all-afternoon activity that you can do with your child. It turns a package of gelatin and a package of marshmallows into a real adventure. And your child will have as much fun eating his creation as he did making it!

Prepare the blue gelatin according to the directions. You may wish to use two packages, depending on the size of the mold you will be using.

Pour $\frac{1}{3}$ of the gelatin mixture into the mold. Have your three-year-old add marshmallows for clouds. Then, put it in the refrigerator to set. (Keep the remaining gelatin at room temperature.)

Each time the gelatin has set, your three-year-old should add more marshmallows, and you should add more gelatin. This will make the clouds appear to be floating in the gelatin sky.

Chill the mixture to set it, remove it carefully from the mold onto a serving dish, and serve it.

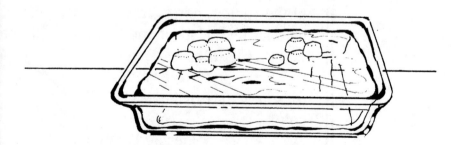

Note: There are many different ways to make gelatin fun. Try blue gelatin with gummy fish for a gelatin aquarium. Try green gelatin with gummy worms for worms in the grass. Try a variety of colors for a rainbow gelatin.

Fast, Easy Candy Cookies

Materials

- Prepared cookie dough
- Candy pieces
- Cookie sheet
- Dull knife
- Plate

Activity

This cookie-making activity can work for anyone—no baking ability required! Use cookie dough from the refrigerator section of your food store. There are two advantages—it is easy for you and there is really no waiting time to bother your impatient three-year-old! My daughter loves adding the candy pieces, and we both love eating the results.

Make buying the ingredients part of the activity. Your three-year-old will feel involved every step of the way. You will need a package of ready-made refrigerated cookie dough. Talk with your child about what kind he would like and look at all the different packages. Let your child help in the decision-making process.

Next, select candy pieces for the tops of the cookies. There are many different kinds you can choose from. (Just make sure to get enough for both of you to sample.)

Read the directions and explain the baking process to your child. This is a good time to stress oven safety.

Place the cookie sheet on a table. Slice the dough and place it on the sheet. You will probably have to do most of the slicing; however, your three-year-old can place the cookies on the sheet and add the candy pieces. Suggest that he try different designs and make patterns or faces on some. Experiment with colors, too.

Bake the cookies and cool them. Then enjoy eating them! You can also make a batch of cookies for gift-giving.

Merry Meals

Materials

- Your favorite cookbooks
- Required ingredients and utensils

Activities

It is always more fun to eat what you help prepare, even for a three-year-old food fussy! Enlist your child's help in preparing these foods, if she seems interested. However, if she is a truly dedicated food-fussy, you may want to prepare them privately so she won't know she is eating something that is good for her. In that case, the three-year-old activity will simply be eating.

For the vegetable hater, grate carrots and make a really yummy carrot cake. Call it a sunshine cake when you serve it.

Or, grate zucchini and make zucchini bread. This is very good spread with cream cheese and jelly and served with apple juice.

The child who turns up her nose at milk will probably eat chocolate pudding made with milk. Put a squirt of whipped cream on top and tell her she can't have it until she finishes her cookies!

Many three-year-olds begin their non-stop days without breakfast because food—especially breakfast food—simply doesn't appeal to them in the morning. Surprise your breakfast-hating three-year-old with oatmeal cookies for breakfast. Make them with raisins for an extra burst of energy.

Note: The parent-on-the-go is probably not eating sensibly either! Take time to sit down and share these merry meals with your three-year-old.

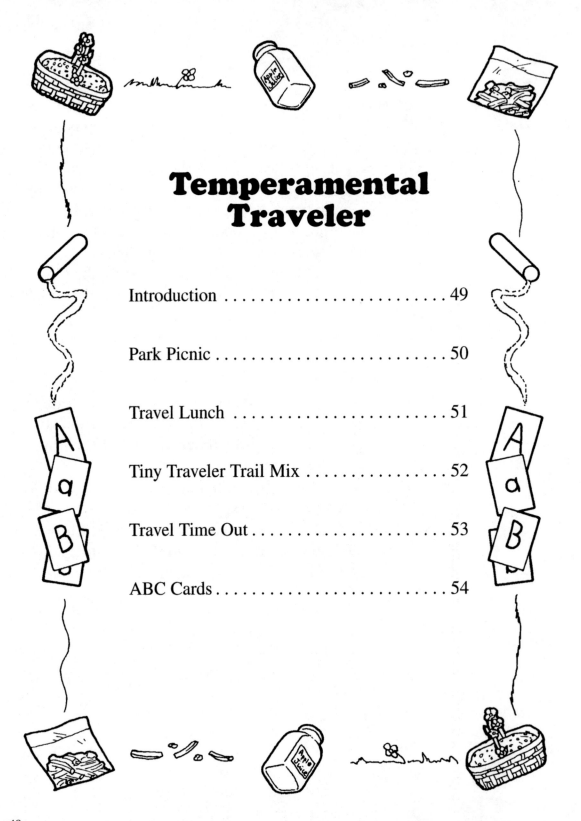

Temperamental Traveler

Introduction

Are We There Yet?

Getting there can be half the fun if you have the right attitude and you are prepared for anything! Getting there with a three-year-old means you must get there on her terms. She has short legs. She needs to go to the potty. She needs a snack. She needs to stop at a park and run around for 20 minutes. She needs her special toy or blanket. She needs a nap. She needs to stop for the day. Traveling with a three-year-old will be fun only if you remember her needs first. The activities in this section have been designed to get you both to your location in one piece.

Rules of the Road

Before you travel with a three-year-old, think about the length of the trip and what you will both need to make it pleasurable. Three-year-olds can be wonderful company. They can often make road trips more enjoyable because they notice things you don't. Three-year-olds like to sing camp songs. They are interested in new experiences. Just remember to pack your patience and away you go!

Tips for Getting There

- Pack your child's favorite toy and blanket. Have spares.
- Use small boxes of juice and plastic bags of cereal for quick energy.
- Pack several favorite and colorful books for your child to look at.
- Pack some baby or child wipes. Paper towels come in handy, too.
- Take a change of clothes for your three-year-old, even if the trip is for the afternoon.
- Hold hands and walk slowly!

Park Picnic

Materials

- Brown bag, lunch box, or picnic basket
- Lunch
- Beverages
- Paper napkins
- Disposable wipes

Activity

When you have a road trip of several hours planned and you know your three-year-old is going to become restless, plan ahead for this "Park Picnic," and your child will have something to look forward to during the ride. Your three-year-old will enjoy helping to put the picnic together, too. Stopping at parks along the way to get some air and run and play has made road trips with my three-year-old fun for both of us!

Talk with your child about your car trip. Tell him where you are going and how long it will take to get there. Decide where you will stop for your picnic. (Or, stop when you both are hungry.)

Plan what you will have in your picnic lunch and put it in together. Let your three-year-old help with this part of the process, even if it is just putting the paper napkins in the lunch box or basket. (See "Travel Lunch" on page 51 for a quick-and-easy travel lunch.)

Remember not to pack any items that can spoil. Make sure all containers are closed tightly and place the lunch away from where little fingers can get into it.

When it is time to stop, find a nice park that has a place to eat. A park with play equipment is an excellent choice. You and your child will leave for the rest of your road trip feeling refreshed.

Think about packing yourself a nice treat, too. Maybe a thermos full of hot coffee or a special sandwich. You need a break in your day as much as your three-year-old does!

Travel Lunch

Materials

- "Tiny Traveler Trail Mix" (See next page.)
- Apple juice in boxes
- Cheese chunks
- Carrot sticks
- Plastic sandwich bags
- Brown paper bag
- Crayons

Activity

A perfect toddler lunch is easy to make, easy to eat, and requires little or no supervision. This "Travel Lunch" can be taken with you wherever you go and consumed by your food-fussy three-year-old. My daughter loves this meal and can eat it anytime—for breakfast, lunch, or dinner.

First, see the next page for the "Tiny Traveler Trail Mix" recipe. Prepare and store this recipe. It can be stored in a plastic container in your cupboard and will last as long as dry cereal lasts.

While you are preparing your three-year-old's lunch, give her the brown paper lunch bag and crayons and ask her to decorate it. This will give you time to put the lunch together and will also personalize the lunch bag for your child.

If your child is taking the lunch to a preschool or day care facility, add a little note with a heart on it and the message "I love you." Show your child this ahead of time and tell her when she looks at it she will know you love her. (A three-year-old will enjoy this more if you explain the note first. As your child gets older and can read, you can put in surprise notes, but as a rule, three-year-olds have enough surprises trying to get through a day.)

Place the lunch ingredients in the bag and you are ready to go. Remember, small children like familiar foods the best!

Tiny Traveler Trail Mix

Materials

- Cheerios®
- Raisins
- Marshmallows
- Chocolate chips
- Dried fruit
- Plastic resealable bags
- Large bowl
- Large spoon

Activity

Traveling can be a fretful time for any three-year-old. Often this is simply a case of low blood sugar. Keep your child happy during travel by making sure he is not hungry. This trail mix can be made ahead and stored in plastic bags. The plastic bag makes it easy for a three-year-old to manage and prevents spills.

Decide what dry ingredients your child likes best and alter the recipe according to his taste. Any bite-size cereal that is not sticky will work. Also consider the weather. For example, chocolate chips are not a good idea if the weather is too hot. Using a large plastic bowl, combine ingredients.

Gently mix the ingredients with a large spoon. Your three-year-old will enjoy doing this part.

Pour ½ cup (120 ml) of trail mix into each small resealable plastic bag.

Experiment with different ingredients. You can use dried cranberries, shredded coconut, butterscotch chips, broken cookie pieces, or whatever you have left over in your cupboard.

Remember, it is best to eat only when your car is not moving. Small children can choke, and they should be supervised when eating. Keep apple juice in boxes available in the car.

Travel Time Out

Materials
- Sidewalk area
- Sidewalk chalk
- Baby wipes

Activity

You have been driving all morning. Your three-year-old is miserable and climbing the walls of your car—thank goodness for the car seat! Pull over to a park or anywhere with a sidewalk and give yourself and your child a creative, relaxing time-out. While this isn't an activity for children in their party clothes, it is an activity for a tired, out-of-sorts traveler and her parent.

Before you go on an all-day road trip, purchase a box of inexpensive sidewalk chalk. You might also want to add baby wipes or kid wipes to this purchase for chalk cleanup on the road.

When you think your three-year-old needs a break, find a sidewalk area. Most parks and all elementary schools will have a sidewalk or other surface (such as blacktop) you can use for chalk drawings.

You might wish to bring a set of chalk clothes for your child to wear during this activity. This way, if you are going somewhere and want to arrive clean, your child can change after the activity and be as good as new when you arrive.

Most three-year-olds will have plenty of ideas about how to use sidewalk chalk, and many will be familiar with it, so it won't be necessary in most cases for you to show your child how to use it.

After the activity, clean up chalky fingers with baby wipes and drive away refreshed and relaxed.

When you see sidewalk chalk that is very inexpensive, it will be helpful to buy several boxes and store an unopened one in the car.

ABC Cards

Materials

- Index cards
- Felt pen

Activity

This activity will keep your three-year-old entertained in the car, and it will also help her become familiar with her ABC's! It is a fun way to make the miles go by more quickly for everyone in the car. This is a sure winner!

Print the letters of the alphabet on index cards, one letter per card. Make sure to make the letters large enough to see easily and make both uppercase and lowercase letters for each letter card.

Show your child the lettered cards before you go on a road trip. Say the letters and show her each card. Eventually, your child will know the letters of the alphabet, but if she doesn't know them until she is in kindergarten or first grade, that is fine. Exposure to letters and numbers is a good thing; just don't insist that she learn them, and she will probably be interested.

When you are on a road trip, tell your child you are going to point out things that start with the letter "A." Hand your child the card to hold and tell her all the things you see that begin with that letter. Repeat the word and say, "That starts with the letter A."

When your child begins to learn the ABC's, you can try asking her to find a sign that has a letter "A." When she does, give her the "A" card. Proceed until she has all the alphabet cards. Give her a small treat for winning.

Note: Be aware that it is best to play this game when another adult is driving and you can sit near your child to hand her the cards. Also, this alphabet games works well if you are entertaining more than one child on a road trip.

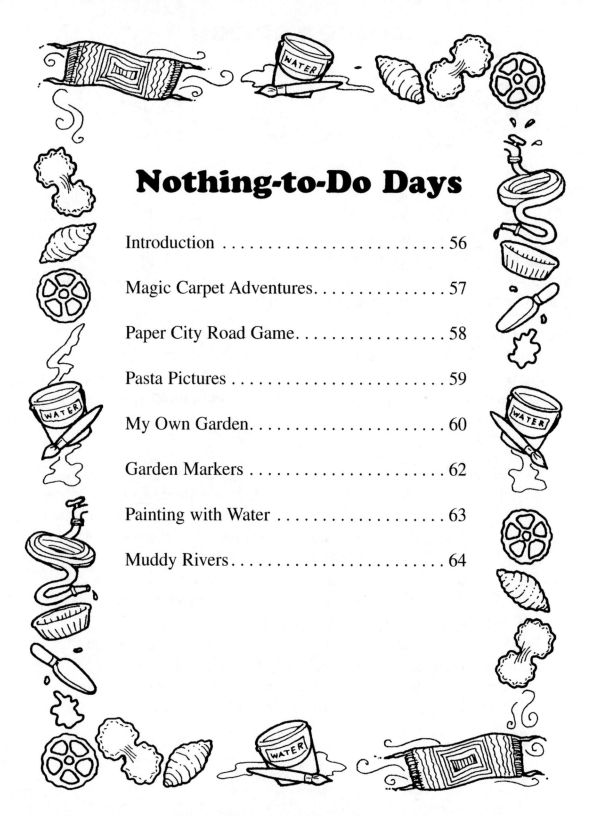

Nothing-to-Do Days

Introduction

There Is Nothing to Do!

The days with nothing to do don't have to be wasted and boring for you or your child. Lazy days with nowhere in particular to be and nothing pressing or urgent at hand can be the beginning of some of your child's favorite memories. The activities in this section are designed for days when you have time to be creative and are relaxed enough to enjoy it.

Creative Time

Nothing-to-do days are great days to put on your oldest clothes and make memories with your three-year-old. Your child will love the special attention he receives and will long remember the fun you both have making something special!

Tips for Nothing-to-Do Days

- Plan ahead. When you know you and your three-year-old will have a stretch of time to do exactly as you both please, review the activities in this section and talk about what might be fun to do. Three-year-olds love to look ahead, plan, and be part of a decision-making team.
- Enjoy yourselves. The days that we all remember the most are the days we spend at relaxed and happy activity. When you are busy and spend much of your time away from your child, it is these long days having fun that you will both look back on, maybe forever.
- Be aware of your child's preferences. If you plan a day hunting for shells and he wants to play sand castles—who cares? Do not become attached to your plans with your three-year-old. It is developmentally appropriate for three-year-olds to go quickly from one activity to another.

Magic Carpet Adventures

Activity

Materials

- Large bath towel
- Imagination

Aladdin had the right idea when he flew on his magic carpet. Children love the fantasy of a magic carpet, and pretending to fly to strange and distant lands with your three-year-old gives you an opportunity for imaginative play in a small space.

Talk about the idea of a magic carpet with your three-year-old. Many young children have seen the Disney movie, *Aladdin.* (My daughter watches it daily—at least it seems that way to me!) Talk about how wonderful it would be to have your own magic carpet to fly anywhere you wanted to go.

Spread an old bath towel or an extra fabric remnant out on your floor and sit with your child on her magic carpet. Discuss where you will be going and what you will see.

As you travel, discuss the sights with your child. Ask questions that require your child to explore language and meaning. When you have seen one destination, choose another and go again!

For additional fun, pack a child's lunch box with picnic foods. My daughter loves to sip apple juice and nibble dry cereal in-flight.

Encourage your child to talk to another family member about the magic carpet game and where you both went by using your imaginations. This gives your child event and sequence recall experience that will later be useful for her in school.

Paper City Road Game

Materials

• Large sheet of paper or cardboard

• Small toys

• Thick-tipped felt pens

Activity

On days with nothing to do, sometimes an easy-to-put-together, quick activity that will interest your three-year-old for hours is a life saver! My three-year-old loves to make roads for her paper city. This makes the activity a little messier and requires more hands-on supervision from you, but whether or not you make constructing the activity part of the fun, your child will spend a lot of time enjoying his "Paper City Road Game."

Get a large piece of butcher paper or split a large cardboard box along the seams to make a flat surface. Or, use a large piece of poster board.

Talk with your child about making a "Paper City Road Game." Help him gather together small toys like cars, action figures, dolls, animals, etc. Talk with him about making a city for his toys. Ask him what kinds of things he would like in his city. Discuss the things that are in a city or town.

Using thick felt pens, help your child draw roads and other areas on his game board. How the game will look will depend on your child's imagination and the toys that will inhabit the city. Remember, there is no right way it should look. Whatever pleases your child and inspires his imagination is the right way to do it!

Encourage your child to add to the fun with blocks. He can build houses, schools, and stores. He can make a bridge across a river, a skyscraper, or a castle. He can make a real city or one from a favorite fairy tale. Make different kinds of games, using different toys. Get out your child's animals and make a farm or use trucks and make a construction site. Play! Join your child or let him play alone. This activity can be used anytime and used again and again. Just store it away and reuse it.

Pasta Pictures

Materials

- Colored pasta
- Construction paper
- White non-toxic glue
- Crayons
- Paper towels
- Newspaper

Activity

Three-year-olds can have added fun after drawing a picture by filling it in with colored pasta shapes. My three-year-old loves to glue anything at all, and this activity is an easy way to let her do something she loves without destroying the house!

Begin by having your child draw a few pictures. Tell her that after she is finished making some pictures she will have a chance to use some glue and other things to make them really pretty. While your child is drawing pictures, color the pasta. (For directions, see "Shoestring Jewelry" on page 31.) Next, pat dry the pasta with paper towels and place it in bowls according to color.

Place the bowls of pasta and the white non-toxic glue on a tray. Cover your child's work area with newspaper.

Show your child how to apply glue and stick pasta shapes onto the picture. After you show her how to do this several times, she will enjoy doing it herself.

After your child has finished a picture, transfer it carefully to a cookie sheet to dry. (Remember not to pick it up quickly or the pasta will fall off and your three-year-old may be very upset.) These pictures can be displayed or even framed when dry.

My Own Garden

Materials

- A place to plant
- Seed packages
- Trowel or shovel
- Watering can

Activity

There are few things more interesting than watching your own garden grow, especially if you have never done it before. Three-year-olds love to have their own little garden. It is an interesting and fascinating activity that can last many days. My three-year-old loves to garden with her grandmother, and it is excellent quality time that she shares with someone very special to her.

The garden activity on this page can be altered to fit your own situation or tastes. It can also be done in an apartment. You don't need a big yard to enjoy a garden! A small sunny part of your garden or even a window sill planter will work great.

Plan your garden with your three-year-old. The best time to do this is when you are actually out getting supplies. Your three-year-old will enjoy picking out seeds and talking about what you are going to do. (Remember, once you gather the materials, your three-year-old will want to start, so be prepared!)

You should probably plan to have the soil prepared ahead of time. Few three-year-olds will have the patience or the physical strength for this process.

Give your child time to browse through the racks of colorful seed packages. Decide whether to plant flowers or vegetables or some of each. Try to pick out something that germinates quickly. (All varieties of beans are very quick to sprout and will grow quickly, especially if you can take the time to soak them overnight before you plant them. If you plan your seed shopping for late afternoon, you can probably talk your three-year-old into soaking the seeds in preparation for planting the next day.)

Read the seed packages to your child and let him see the word that tells the name of the flower or vegetable

My Own Garden *(cont.)*

you are planting. Then show him how to use the trowel or the shovel and the watering can. Give him some time to practice. (Remember to wear old clothes. It is fun to have special clothes to wear just for gardening!)

Decide how the rows of seeds are going to go and let your child help you with the actual planting. Some three-year-olds will have a hard time with a shovel, but they can usually drop seeds into holes. (Remind your child that seeds never go in his mouth and be aware of this possibility.)

After the seeds are planted, show your child how to carefully water the new garden. Talk with him about how he must water the garden every day so the seeds will begin to grow.

Use the "Garden Marker Activity" on the next page to make colorful markers for your child's garden. This will give him something interesting to do while he is waiting for his garden to grow.

Garden Markers

Materials

- Craft sticks or tongue depressors
- White thick paper
- Clear contact paper
- Crayons
- Empty seed packages
- Scissors
- White non-toxic glue

Activity

Your three-year-old will enjoy making these easy-to-do markers for her garden. They will be useful in marking the areas of her garden and reminding both of you what she has planted and where it is. This activity also gives your child something useful and interesting to do while she waits for her seeds to sprout.

Cut thick paper or poster board in 11-inch x 4-inch (28 cm. x 10 cm.) strips. Fold it in half so the marker is 5½ inches x 4 inches (14 cm. x 10 cm.), double with a fold at the top.

Using the saved seed packages as a guide, have your three-year-old draw a picture of each kind of plant on each folded piece of poster board. (You can also find pictures of flowers or vegetables in gardening or cookbooks to use as a guide.)

After your child has finished the drawing, open the poster board and coat the inside with glue. Refold it, placing a stick inside the fold. (Later this stick will hold up the marker when you push it into the ground in the garden.) Press under a stack of books or other heavy object overnight.

Next, cover the marker with clear contact paper. This will keep the marker dry in the garden when your child waters or when it rains. These markers will not last forever; however, the contact paper should keep them in shape until the seeds sprout and often longer.

Let your child place the finished markers in her garden to mark each kind of seed.

Painting with Water

Materials

- Paintbrushes or rollers
- Buckets
- Water
- Old clothing

Activity

Painting with water is an activity that can provide hours of good, clean fun. It is easy; it can be done anywhere you have a stretch of cement, sidewalk, fence, or wall. It is an activity that involves both the large and small muscle groups, a necessary factor in your child's appropriate development at age three.

Find an outdoor space with something that your three-year-old can paint. Just be sure that your child's play space is safe from traffic and other potential dangers.

Fill a bucket with water and show your child how to dip her brush and paint. The water will make a nice painted surface, and your child will be able to see the areas she has already painted. On a hot day, her painted area will dry, and she will be able to do it again. (This activity can take a lot of time.)

Encourage your child to make designs, write letters, and explore all of the different things she can do with her water paints. Be prepared to get wet and to have your child get wet. That is part of the fun, and on a very hot day it will cool you both down!

During this activity, you can talk about how water evaporates, how heat feels, and how it is cooler in the shade. Three-year-olds are interested in their surroundings and can begin to grasp many ideas about natural science which will help them later in school.

Also, try getting your shoes or your bare feet wet and making tracks with your three-year-old. Talk about the concepts of big and little.

Muddy Rivers

Activity

This is a perfect activity for those lazy days with nothing to do, and it is only for people who don't mind getting muddy. One of the great joys of early childhood is playing in the mud. So, when you have nothing better to do one day, let your three-year-old get really muddy! Have a wonderful time and finish up with a warm bath with lots of bubbles!

Remember! Whenever your child is playing with or around water, even from a hose, there is danger of drowning. While most of us played in the mud when we were little and nothing happened, it is important to be aware of safety precautions.

Find a space in your yard that you do not care about. This space should be near a hose. Gather digging tools as well as some old pie pans and other mud-pie-making kinds of tools, if you wish.

Talk with your child about making a river or a lake. Use a trowel to dig a few inches in a line so that when you add water it will have somewhere to go. Show your child how to make a hole at the end for a lake. Your three-year-old will be able to use a trowel to dig but may need lots of practice. To make this part of the activity longer, don't add water until the very end.

Add rocks or other materials around the lake and river or drag out some of your child's less precious action figures and other toys to make river inhabitants.

Remember, having tactile and bodily-kinesthetic hands-on activities is good for your child and developmentally sound. Also, an older sibling makes a great mate for this activity—and you won't have to get muddy!

Materials
- Dirt
- Hose
- Old clothes
- Trowels and other tools

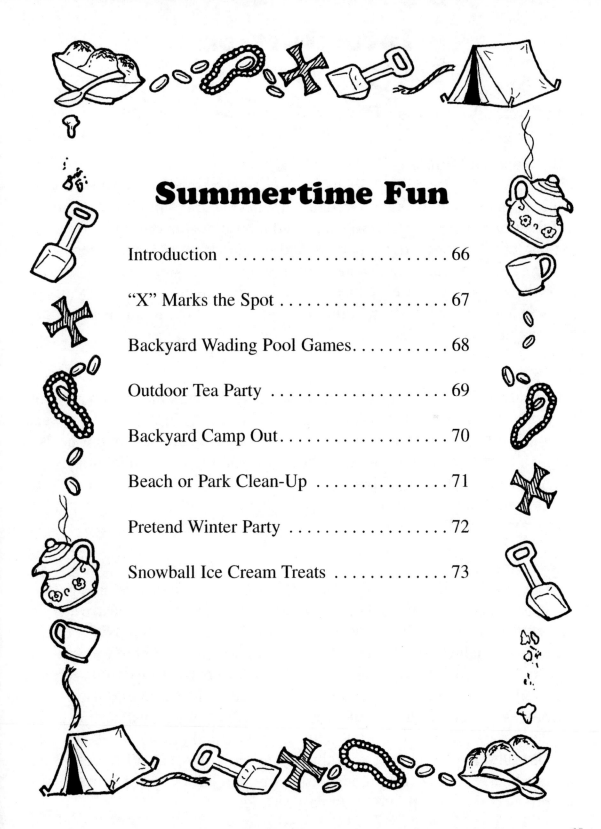

Summertime Fun

Introduction

In the Good Old Summertime

Don't we all love summer? Picnics, beaches, watermelon, fireworks, vacations, and fun in the sun! Or, does summer seem too hot, too crowded, too full of expensive day trips to over-rated amusement parks, and a three-year-old who is over-tired, sunburned, and in tears from too much merry-making? Summer can be all of these things, and the key to surviving it happily is simplicity. Three-year-olds can spend a great deal of happy time at simple activities, and you will find it can reduce your stress if you reduce your summertime expectations.

Have Fun in the Summertime

How can we, as parents of three-year-olds, juggle work and summer? Not many of us have the luxury of a summertime break. At best, we have a week or two of vacation. Yet, we all feel as if we would like to kick up our heels and get a little more of the summertime feeling and fun that childhood summers used to produce. This section has been designed to provide amusing and fun memories for your child, and give you, as a weary parent, a little of the joy and relaxation that you once associated with summer!

Tips for Summertime Fun

- Remember, safety first! Be aware of the safety hazards that could affect your three-year-old. NEVER leave your child unattended near water, whether the ocean, lake, swimming pool, or even a wading pool. Even if your small child is water-safe, you must watch him in the water.
- Don't overdo. During summer it's easier for your three-year-old to get overly tired and even exhausted or dehydrated. Make sure to pack bottles of water or juice. Be aware of the signs of heat exhaustion and dehydration and do not ask too much of your child in hot weather.
- Use sunscreen to protect your three-year-old's skin. Don't forget insect repellent, either. Check the labels before purchasing to see if the products are appropriate for three-year-olds.

"X" Marks the Spot

Activities

The beach is the perfect place for you and your three-year-old to have an imaginary game of pirates. My three-year-old (Captain Daisy) actually created this beach or sandbox activity, and we have spent many enjoyable hours on the beach hiding and marking our own buried treasure.

Simply gather "treasure" with your child on the sand or in a sandbox. Treasure can be anything she thinks is worth calling treasure—rocks, shells, twigs, or small toys that you bring along. Then, play "pirates." As one pirate hides the treasure by digging a hole and marking it with an "X," the other pirate sneaks over and steals the buried treasure. Or, be a gang of pirates and work together. Your child will have a lot of ideas. You can take direction once the imaginative play begins.

Remember, this pirate fun will get you both out in the sun for long periods of time. Pretend your sun hats are pirate hats and be sure to wear sunscreen.

Materials

- Beach or sandbox
- Shells, rocks, or sandbox toys

Backyard Wading Pool Games

Materials

- Backyard area
- Wading pool
- Hose and faucet
- Sunscreen
- Towels
- Plastic containers
- Boats or water toys
- Imagination
- Outdoor slide (Optional)

Activities

A backyard wading pool can make a whole summertime full of inexpensive and memorable fun. There's no reason to lament the absence of a real pool or try to pack up everything and everyone for an afternoon at the beach. With a minimum investment and a little imagination, you can make your own backyard vacation wonderland. Your three-year-old will have just as much fun as she would for far more money at a resort, and you will have an excuse to play in a wading pool, splash, build sand castles, and otherwise join with your three-year-old in your own backyard vacation.

Note: Children must ALWAYS be supervised when playing in or around water, even from a hose or wading pool.

Your three-year-old will enjoy almost any kind of water activity. Here are a few easy-to-do examples:

- Use different-sized plastic cups and bowls to transfer water back and forth.
- Float plastic fish and pretend to fish.
- Use a bubble mixture to blow bubbles while you are wading.
- Place a plastic slide into the pool and have a water slide.
- Have pre-swimmers practice holding breath and blowing bubbles.
- Use plastic balls for water catch.
- Pretend to be deep-sea divers, dolphins, fish, mermaids and mermen, underwater explorers, and scientists.
- Move your portable sandbox near your water area and make a beach.
- Use squirt guns for water play.
- Have a boat race.
- Remember to use sunscreen, and empty the pool completely before leaving the area.

Outdoor Tea Party

Materials

- Tea party food (cookies, small sandwiches, fruit, juice)
- Napkins
- Table cloth
- Stuffed animals (Optional)

Activity

Three-year-olds love parties, and tea parties are no exception. Since Alice in Wonderland sat down for her first cup of tea, small children have served pretend tea to their dolls and teddy bears. Use this idea as an opportunity to practice party manners, as well as pitching in to clean up!

Talk to your child about having a tea party. Investigate your kitchen cupboards together. Let your child plan the menu (with your help) and take part in the preparations. Be prepared for your child to do more preparing than eating!

Decide with your child where she would like to have the party and how many guests (both real and imaginary) will be invited. If she wants to have guests at the party, help her decide which stuffed animals or dolls she would like to have attend. (This is also an excellent time to invite Grandma or Grandpa, Daddy, or Uncle to the festivities.)

Let your child set the table and enjoy!

Backyard Camp Out

Materials

- Tent
- Sleeping Bags
- Barbecue
- Marsh-mallows
- Long forks or roasting tools
- Camping gear
- Insect repellent

Activity

Camping doesn't have to be a difficult and tedious experience with your three-year-old. In fact, a weekend night at home can feel like a real camp out when you have it in your own backyard. My three-year-old daughter thinks this is a real adventure! We sing songs, roast marshmallows, and act like real campers.

You might want to watch a video like *Barney's Campfire Sing-Along first*. Or, go to a camping supply store and browse. Talk with your child about the different kinds of camping supplies and what you will use for your own camp out.

Decide ahead of time how elaborate your camp out will be. You might want to pack sandwiches and other no-cook treats, or simply start your camp out after dinner. Or, plan a barbecue. Remember to watch your child carefully around fire and hot surfaces.

You can even bring out your guitar or sing simple camp songs. Lie on sleeping bags and look at the night sky and the stars. Talk about the moon and the Earth and the planets with your child. Listen to the night sounds. See how many you can name.

Do your best to get a good night's sleep and don't be surprised if your camp out moves indoors sometime in the middle of the night. Remember that even though you are at home, insect repellent is a good idea to prevent bites.

Beach or Park Clean-Up

Materials

- Trash bags
- Littered area

Activity

Even three-year-olds can begin to feel responsible for the world around them. This clean-up activity gives three-year-olds a real and do-able way to make a difference. Talk with your child about how he can make a difference by learning to pick up litter in your local park or beach area. This activity is an excellent way for you to begin talking about recycling and the earth, in a way that is both age-appropriate and hands-on.

After trying a litter pick-up with your three-year-old, make it a regular part of your park or beach visits. Give your child positive feedback about what a good job he is doing to make the Earth a nicer, cleaner place for everyone.

Also, if you decide to recycle with your child, you might want to let him start a piggy bank and later a small savings account with the money from these recycling efforts.

Pretend Winter Party

Materials

- Holiday video tapes
- Holiday tree
- Construction paper
- Ribbon
- Glue
- Tape
- Scissors

Activity

Christmas in July? Why not? When it's too hot and the usual summer fun has worn off, have a winter party indoors! Use a holiday theme, or just pretend it's cold outside. My three-year-old loves Christmas so much that she enjoys pretending it's Christmas almost anytime. This activity is a nice break from the usual summer fun and sure to please (and cool down) everyone!

Crank up the air conditioner and decorate a pretend holiday tree. (Make one from construction paper or use a large indoor plant.) Use ribbons, bows, and paper chains for decoration, or dig into your regular holiday decorations and borrow some for the day.

Watch holiday videos and listen to seasonal music. Sing along to your favorite holiday tunes and remember the fun you had last winter.

Prepare the "Snowball Treats" described on the next page and have a party. Make Christmas cookies or a mini Hanukkah feast and enjoy. You can even make or buy small, inexpensive gifts to exchange with each other.

Snowball Ice Cream Treats

Materials

- Vanilla ice cream
- Shredded coconut
- Cookie sheet
- Ice cream scooper
- Dinner plate
- Serving plates
- Two tablespoons
- Candles (Optional)
- Matches (Optional)

Activity

These snowball treats are yummy and easy to make! Your three-year-old will be able to really help and feel excited about the results. They'll make a great addition to the "Pretend Winter Party" on page 72 or can be used anytime for a tasty snack.

Clear a kitchen work space that is accessible to your child. Gather the materials and have them all together in one place for easy access. Remember, once you start working with ice cream, you will have to move quickly so you won't end up with soup!

Set out a cookie sheet for the finished products and fill a dinner plate with shredded coconut.

Prepare the ice cream by cutting it into cubes (or scooping it from a container with an ice cream scoop). Vanilla ice cream in a rectangular cardboard carton will make it possible to cut the ice cream quickly with a knife into cubes that will be easy to roll in the coconut.

Place each scoop or square of ice cream in the coconut and roll. Use tablespoons to roll the ice cream and completely cover each scoop or square with coconut. Remove the balls and place them on the cookie sheet. Freeze them until ready to serve. You can place a candle in each snowball and serve them with the lights turned low for extra effect. You can also try different flavors of ice cream or different toppings for other effects. Chocolate ice cream with chocolate sprinkles is one interesting variation.

Places to Go with a Three-Year-Old

Look at the list below and see how many you have tried. Consider the experiences you have had with your three-year-old in a new way. Remember, each time your three-year-old has a real experience in the world, it is increasing his development in a positive way. Each experience you have with your child adds to his knowledge base, vocabulary, and overall ability to learn.

- The supermarket
- A produce stand
- A farm
- A department store
- A discount store
- A toy store
- A craft store
- A government building
- The bank
- A fire station
- Your office
- A children's library
- An adults' library
- The zoo
- A children's museum
- An adults' museum
- A playground
- Any park
- A field

- A forest
- The mountains
- A river
- A hotel
- A restaurant
- An aquarium
- The beach or lake shore
- A look at the moon
- An amusement park
- A swimming pool
- A gym
- A children's theater
- A movie theater
- A puppet show
- A pony ride
- A police station
- An elementary school (for "big kids")

- An outdoor sculpture garden
- An airport
- An airplane
- A train station
- A train
- A bus
- A taxi
- A subway
- A boat
- A construction site
- A post office
- An ice cream or frozen yogurt store
- A sunset watch
- A trip to the snow
- A pile of leaves
- Anywhere you go without him regularly and talk about

All of the places listed above are places you can go with a three-year-old where he won't break anything or get in the way or get in trouble. Look for places where your child can learn something new or become acquainted with people outside your family and the usual group of friends. Police and fire fighters are usually very positive about meeting children. Call ahead for details if you aren't sure a certain experience would be appropriate for your child.

The Best Activity— Communication

The main ingredient in all of the activities described in this book is the communication between you and your child. The more we talk to our children, the more quickly they learn and the faster they develop intellectually.

It has been proven time and time again by medical and educational professionals that children who are spoken to—and listened to—regularly have a much easier time making friends, learning, being able to say "no" to peer pressure, and developing into emotionally healthy, productive adults.

Communication Tips

- LISTEN to your three-year-old. Three-year-olds are not just repeating words and telling stories that have only to do with their own fantasies. If you give your three-year-old a chance to talk to you on a regular basis, you will find she has opinions, she reacts to the world around her, she likes and dislikes things and people, and she can often tell you the reasons for her choices.

- DEVOTE some time without activities to your child every day. Take time to just co-exist in a relaxed way with your child. Watch her. See how she sees the world. Often your three-year-old will give you a new way of looking at things. Children see things we don't notice anymore—shapes of clouds, bugs in the grass, special flowers, people's faces. As adults we are too often busy mentally with our own concerns every second of the day. As a result, we miss a lot that our children can help us see.

- CHECK in with your child's preschool. Sit in for several days and drop in unannounced. Watch how the professional care givers care for your child and other children. Notice how they relate to the children, how they speak to them, and whether they listen. An important part of your child's ability to communicate isn't just your personal communication with her but also the communication styles of the other adults who play primary roles in her life.

- LOVE your three-year-old every day and let her know it. Demonstrations of love make children stronger, more capable adults.

Bibliography of Resources

Brazelton, T. Berry, M.D., *Touchpoints: Your Child's Emotional and Behavioral Development.* Addison Wesley Publishing, 1992.

Briggs, D. *Your Child's Self Esteem.* Doubleday, 1970.

Eisenberg, A., Murkoff, H., & Hathaway, S. *What to Expect in the Toddler Years.* Workman Publishing, 1994.

Galinsky, E., & David, J. *The Preschool Years.* Ballantine, 1988.

Kersey, Ed.D., K. *The Art of Sensitive Parenting.* Berkley Books, 1994.

Shelov, M.D., F.A.A.P., S. *Caring For Your Baby and Young Child: Birth to Age Five.* Bantam Books, 1993.

Bibliography of Children's Books

Bridwell, N. *Clifford at the Circus.* Scholastic, Inc., 1985.

Bridwell, N. *Clifford's Good Deeds.* Scholastic, Inc., 1985.

Carter, N. *Where's My Fuzzy Blanket?* Scholastic, Inc., 1991.

Carter, N. *Where's My Squishy Ball?* Scholastic, Inc., 1993.

Hill, E. *Spot Goes to the Circus.* G.P. Putman's Sons, 1986. Other excellent Eric Hill books include *Spot Goes to the Farm, Spot Goes to the Park,* and *Spot's Birthday Party.*

Hutchings, T. *Little Woolly Lamb.* McClanahan Book Company, Inc., 1990.

Lowell, S. *The Tortoise and the Jackrabbit.* Northland Publishing, 1994.

Martin, Jr., B. *Chicka Chicka Boom Boom.* Simon & Schuster, 1989.

Ruschak, L. *The Counting Zoo.* Aladdin Books, 1992.

Sloboder, B. *Who Said That?* Grosset & Dunlap, 1993.

Speed, T. *Crawly Bug and the Firehouse Pie.* Newfield Publications, Inc., 1993.

Waddell, M., & B. Firth. *Can't You Sleep, Little Bear?* Candlewick Press, 1988.

Waddell, M. *Owl Babies.* Candlewick Press, 1992.

Bibliography of Sing-Along Videos

Kidsongs Series (Kidvision), a division of Warner Entertainment. Some of the best include the following:

- *A Day at Old MacDonald's Farm*, 1985.
- *Play Along Songs*, 1993.
- *Country Sing-Along*, 1995.
- *Baby Animal Songs*, 1995.
- *Very Silly Songs*, 1991.

Sesame Street Videos, Random House Home Video. All of the Sesame Street videos are excellent! Some of our favorites include the following:

- *Monster Hits,* 1990.
- *Rock and Roll*, 1990.
- *Sing Yourself Silly*, 1990.
- *We All Sing Together*, 1993.

Kidvision, a division of Warner Entertainment. Some of the best include the following:

- *Bulldozer Songs*, 1995.
- *Train Songs*, 1995.
- *Firetruck Songs*, 1995.

Viacom International, Inc., a division of Sony Music.

- *Sing Along with Binyah Binyah.* Gullah Gullah Island, 1995.
- *Sing Along with Eureeka.* Eureeka's Castle, 1995.